HELL HAD TO LET ME GO

Divine Purpose and Destiny Called My Name

Antoinette Barnwell

WestBow
PRESS®
A DIVISION OF THOMAS NELSON
& ZONDERVAN

WestBow Press books may be ordered through booksellers or by contacting:

WestBow Press
A Division of Thomas Nelson & Zondervan
1663 Liberty Drive
Bloomington, IN 47403
www.westbowpress.com
844-714-3454

Scripture taken from the King James Version of the Bible.

Scripture quotations marked (NLT) are taken from the Holy Bible, New Living Translation, copyright ©1996, 2004, 2015 by Tyndale House Foundation. Used by permission of Tyndale House Publishers, a Division of Tyndale House Ministries, Carol Stream, Illinois 60188. All rights reserved.

Scripture taken from the Holy Bible, NEW INTERNATIONAL VERSION®. Copyright © 1973, 1978, 1984, 2011 by Biblica, Inc. All rights reserved worldwide. Used by permission. NEW INTERNATIONAL VERSION® and NIV® are registered trademarks of Biblica, Inc. Use of either trademark for the offering of goods or services requires the prior written consent of Biblica US, Inc.

Scripture taken from the New King James Version. Copyright © 1979, 1980, 1982 by Thomas Nelson, Inc. Used by permission. All rights reserved.

ISBN: 978-1-6642-3023-1 (sc)
ISBN: 978-1-6642-3024-8 (e)

Print information available on the last page.

WestBow Press rev. date: 6/24/2021

CONTENTS

INTRODUCTION

The biblical story of Hosea and Gomer captivated me the first time I read it.

Only God's infinite wisdom and witty sense of humor, would use the collaboration of two unlikely people; a prophet and a prostitute, to fulfill bible prophecy.

Biblical scripture reminds us though, that despite our flaws and weakness, God can and will use anyone and anything, to bring him glory.

He often uses the foolish things of this world to confound the wise. So he alone will get the glory from our life.

God used the lives and story of Hosea and Gomer, to provoke the message of repentance for sin, from his chosen people, the Isrealites.

Hosea and Gomer's story, is a comparison or an analogy of God; in this case God; being Israel's husband. Whose wife, Israel, or bride; have left him, and turned away from her first love; God, to worship idols, in the form of people or things, other than God, therefore, committing adultery.

Hosea's marriage to Gomer displays God's patience with his people. In regard to sin and how far he will extend grace and mercy towards us, because he loves us.

With the hope of turning our hearts towards his will for our life and ultimately bringing us back to him, to love.

Hosea was a devoted Prophet of God. During the time he and Gomer lived, the country was in total chaos.

Murder and robbery was the norm and people were forced into bondadge and slavery.

The judges and priests that ruled and in charge of keeping order among the people, were corrupt and greedy.

They devoted themselves to gods they could make for their benefit. Leading them to worship God and their idol, Baal, on the same altar.

God had provided everything the Isrealites needed during their years of captivity and slavery in Egypt, and during the forty years they spent in the wilderness.

For example, God fed them food daily, in the form of manna and quail and gave them water to drink.

He guided them during the day with a pillar of cloud; and at night, with a pillar of fire.

Their clothes and shoes never wore out. God kept his people safe from danger and harm and none of them were sick.

The Isrealites experienced no lack in any area of their life because of God's goodness. Instead, they murmured and complained and lived their lives outside of his covenant.

God is still providing for his children today. He wants us to trust him to supply our every need and to have a grateful heart when he does it.

God inhabits the praises of his people. When we murmur and complain, we stop his blessings, his very best, from freely flowing in our lives.

ANTOINETTE BARNWELL

The nation we currently live in was founded on the principles and morals of God's word, the bible. Which included prayer in our schools.

Sin and our desire to live according to what we feel is right and not according to God's word, have brought many to the conclusion; we no longer need God. How untrue.

God stated in his word in, (2 Timothy: 3: 1-5) (KJV),

In the last days, men would become lovers of themselves, covetous, boasters, proud, blasphemers, disobedient to parents, unthankful and unholy.

In 2021, we don't have to look far to see these examples God gave, being openly displayed in our world.

Just like during the time Hosea and Gomer lived.

People no longer have a reverential fear of God. Even at church. This is why in many churches, the immoral lifestyles and values accepted by the world, are openly welcomed and displayed in the church.

There's no longer a distinction between the world and the church.

Allowing Satan the platform he needs, to use demon possesed men and women, to carry out his satanic plans.

Giving them the freedom to walk inside of our churches, pull out a hand gun, to murder people, with no care at all.

Our churches have become venues for entertainment. Promoting our selfish agendas. Treated like businesses. Not the hospitals God intended them to be.

Christians are to be Ambassadors for Christ. Displaying his attributes through the fruit of the spirit. In action and deed.

Being salt and light, this dark world needs and is longing to receive. Welcoming all people into God's Kingdom, with open arms.

Showing unconditional love to the emotionally sick. Those who have lost their way, those feeling hopeless, and are ready to give up on life.

Letting them know they are not discarded goods, as seen by the world. That they are valuable and loved by God. In Spite of their sin.

As a people, we've failed God miserably, but because of his never ending mercy and love for us, he says in,

(2 Chronicles 7:14) (KJV),

If my people, who are called by my name, Shall humble themselves and pray, and seek my face, and turn from their wicked ways; then will I hear from heaven, and I will heal their land.

As long as we have breath in our physical bodies, that same God pleading to the Isrealites, during Hosea and Gomer's generation, is alive and well today.

He's still calling out to us and whosoever will receive him.

This includes all people; Jews and Gentiles. All in need of a Savior.

I personally know God, the creator of our universe, to be a loving and caring father.

Who walks with me daily. Twenty-four hours a day, seven days a week. He's never too busy to hear me when I call him.

He's a father who's concerned about the smallest details of our lives and because he's all powerful, he has the ability and power to turn everything the devil meant for evil in our lives, and work it together for our good. (Romans 8:28) (KJV)

God wants us to repent from the sin that separates us from him. Commit to living for him and he will always forgive our sins.

He will never condemn us but willingly receive us into his family. What an awesome God and Savior he is.

If you don't know him as your heavenly father and personal Lord and Savior, you're missing out!

Today can be your day! Right where you are, you can receive God's free gift of salvation. By accepting his son, Jesus Christ.

Ask Jesus to forgive you of your sins. To come and live in your heart, and he will do it.

It's as simple as that. Don't worry about what's wrong in your life because he already knows.

His death at Calvary's Cross, made provision for every mistake you and I made in our past, present, and will make in the future.

The abundant, free, joy-filled, peaceful life Jesus died to give you, awaits you.

Receive it today and it's yours. You will never regret it.

CHAPTER 1

Your Brokenness Can't Stop Your God Given Destiny

The text in Jeremiah 1:5, (NIV),

Explains it this way, before I formed you in the womb, I knew you. Before you were born I set you apart; I appointed you a prophet to the nations.

This lets us know that before we are born, our destiny and purpose is planned by God, our creator and is connected to his master plan for humanity.

We all have the choice to either walk in the awesome destiny and purpose God planned for us, or choose to walk in the path we've created for ourselves.

God's will for us is perfect. The plans and choices we make for ourselves, God will permit, but when we disobey him, our plans will never bring us his sweet peace, true fulfillment, and the great rewards that come with being in his perfect will.

Hosea's obedience to God, without question, when God told him to marry Gomer, allowed God's divine plan for humanity to be fulfilled.

What a testament to Hosea. Knowing the persecution he'd experience, by being obedient to God.

God gave Hosea and Gomer names with specific purpose and meaning. Hosea's name means; salvation.

Gomer's name means; complete.

What a contrast to the life Gomer was forced to live.

The wickedness in the kings and priests hearts, that ruled during the period Gomer lived, forced all of the beautiful women in the country, into a life of prostitution for their profit. Because of this, Gomer was ordered to work as a temple dancer and a prostitute.

Imagine the emotional pain and identity issues associated with a profession she did not solicit.

A profession looked down upon and frowned upon by society.

Emotionally stamping her spirit with immense pain. Having to conquer her entire life.

In addition to socially wearing a physical label.

One that Forces the guilty to wear masks. Masks covering spirits of oppression and depression.

Masks of :

SHAME:

(Psalm: 34:35), (KJV),

Jesus Christ is our shield, our glory and the lifter of our head.

We no longer have to walk in the guilt of our past or feel condemned when we sin. Living our lives with our head hung down.

Jesus Christ took our shame and guilt when he died on the cross.

Our sins are forgiven because of the blood sacrifice he made on the cross for you and I.

Jesus Christ, the spotless lamb of God, who never sinned. Was the only one, who could pay the sin debt we owed to God.

Thank you Jesus for your love and sacrifice for me.

When we miss the mark, by not keeping God's commandments, God's word; the bible, convicts us, and reminds us that through salvation, we are now empowered by Christ, to overcome sin and we no longer have to be bound or enslaved by it.

SADNESS:

Psalm 34: 18 (KJV),

Our God is close to us when our heart and spirit are broken.

On days when everything in our lives seems to be going wrong and we see no solution to our problems.

God promised to never leave or forsake us and he's a promise keeper.

When we feel sad, that's the time we should run to God, our heavenly father, and seek his presence. Not away from God.

Magnify his great love for us and his awesome power and majesty.

As we worship and adore him, spirits of oppression and depression, sent by the devil, have to flee.

FEAR:

When we're fearful and feeling afraid, God says, fear not; for I am with you, be not dismayed; for I am your God; I will strengthen you; yea I will uphold you with my righteous right hand.

(Isaiah 41:10)(KJV),

God does not give us a spirit of fear, but of power, love, and of a sound mind. (2 Timothy 1:7)(KJV)

Until we take our last breath, the devil will use the spirit of fear to try to paralyze us and to stop us from making progress in the things of God.

When we feel the spirit of fear present, begin speaking the word of God out loud. In the area the enemy is using fear, to torment us.

Speak God's word until it becomes tangible in our life. Something personal we can hold on to.

We must also make a sound decision to believe what God's word says about us and not what the circumstances and symptoms appear to be.

REJECTION:

Psalm 27:10 (KJV),

Even if my father and my mother forsake me, then the Lord will take me up.

People whom we love, will sooner or later, turn their back on us and in some way disappoint us. Because of the sin nature we inherited from Adam and Eve.

We can always count on God to be there when we need him. He's only a prayer away, and he will never let us down.

I imagine Gomer experiencing these emotions, while working as a prostitute; preparing to meet the men, who paid for her services.

Longing to hear them speak comforting words of affirmation. Telling her she's beautiful, how they've longed to be in her presence, that she's awesome and wonderful. Unlike no other woman in the world.

Words spoken to her by strangers. Words permeating her soul, and temporarily medicating her emotional wounds and scars.

After each encounter, reality sets in, and Gomer is reminded that this is only a mirage. Not her reality.

Her reality is, she has a family awaiting her at home. A husband, children and chores to attend to. Responsibilities that come along with having a family.

Emotionally and physically, Gomer is stuck in this wayward place.

Her need to fulfill the emotional pain and emptiness she's feeling inside, is more important to her, than accepting the normalcy and satisfaction of being a wife to her husband and a mother to her children.

Her family loves her, needs her, and is counting on her to be there for them. Because she's stuck in this wayward place, she can't be everything they need and want her to be.

Most of us have never experienced Gomer's actual life, but we've all dealt with negative emotions and have felt stuck in life, because of the deck of cards, life dealt us.

Paths in life we wouldn't have voluntarily walked. Dealing with difficult choices and circumstances, as a result of our immature decisions or bad life decisions made by people whom we are connected to.

Situations that leave us to cope with feelings of emptiness, unworthiness, hopelessness and seeing no way out.

Satan, our spiritual enemy, will never give up trying to defeat us. He's spent years studying our lives and daily patterns.

He knows our personal vice of choice. The things he used to trip us up in the past.

As long as we stay connected to sin; manifested through addictions and ungodly habits and soul ties, Satan will continue to use them.

His ultimate goal is to derail us off of God's perfect will and destiny for our life.

There are many things Satan may use to be a distraction in our lives. Your vice may manifest itself through alcohol, sex, drugs, food, achieving more money or personal status. To the point of never experiencing the fulfillment you hoped for.

Just remember that at the end of the day, none of these things will ever give us the true fulfillment we're seeking.

Only God, in his special way, can fill the hollow void in our spirit.

Healing starts through a personal relationship, with his son, Jesus Christ. Jesus Christ said in, (John 10:10) (KJV),

The thief comes only to steal, kill and destroy; I came so they would have life and it more abundantly.

It doesn't matter what background or past you came from or the mistakes you've made in life.

God made you and I in his image. We are perfectly and wonderfully made.

God loves us and accepts us and wants to do miraculous things for us and through us.

CHAPTER 2

The Destiny And Purpose God Placed On The Inside Of Us, Is Meant To Impact And Change The World

I believe the Covid-19 pandemic we're experiencing, that started in March of 2020, God allowed. To give us all a global wakeup call.

God's message to his people is: I've blessed you, protected you and never left or forsake you.

Despite my faithfulness to you, you've placed other gods before me.

You've made idols out of government officials, sports figures, people in the arts and entertainment industry, family and physical gifts I've given you.

Your lust and greed to obtain more money, have become a major distraction in your lives.

Forgetting that it is I, who gave you the power to get wealth. To establish my covenant on the earth.

The gifts and talents God placed on the inside of us, were given to us, to make an impact in the world we live in, and to bring him glory.

As long as we put God first, while operating in our gifts and callings, morally and according to God's word, God will allow them to produce Kingdom expansion and growth.

The Seven Pillars of Influence, God created, will always be corrupt, when we live our lives contrary to the bible.

Our spiritual blindness has allowed Satan to infiltrate his way into these institutions creating havoc. Through corrupt men and women, used by him.

Christians operating in these systems with integrity and morality, will reverse Satan's plans; to kill, steal and destroy.

The presence of God operating in these institutions, will shift the environment of our world.

Displaying the love of God, with unity, integrity, productivity and prosperity.

Just as God intended them to be.

THE SEVEN PILLARS OF INFLUENCE ARE:

1). BUSINESS:

God was the first businessman. In the first chapter of Genesis, God thoughtfully created the heavens and the earth.

Providing everything the occupants living in it would need. He included; the heavens above; the stars, moon and sun. The oceans, vegetation and animals.

After he finished making it all, God said it was good. Because nothing he creates lacks anything.

God then made the man and woman.

He then placed Adam and Eve in the garden and instructed them to maintain, and rule the garden with dominion and authority and to be fruitful and multiply.

This text lets us know that our God; the creator of all things, is a strategic planner and he does nothing without thoroughly thinking it through.

Our proof that from the beginning, God always had our best interest at heart.

Because we are made in God's image, we have God's creative ability on the inside of us.

He showed us this in, (Genesis 2:19-20),(KJV),

when he told Adam to name all of the animals he created, and he did it.

As a child of God, destined by God, to work in the business field, begin to walk in the dominion and authority God gave you.

Let your creative abilities flow. They're inventions and ideas, lying dormant on the inside of you and are waiting to come out.

Kingdom brands that the world has never seen.

That God's going to use, to bless his kingdom, and he wants to do it through you.

God is waiting to change the world through you. What are you waiting on? The world needs your gifts.

2). RELIGION:

(2 Timothy 4:3), (KJV), States,

For a time will come when people will no longer listen to sound and wholesome teaching.

They will follow their own desires and will look for teachers who will tell them what they want to hear.

Despite what the world teaches, and the different doctrines being preached today, Jesus Christ is the only way to access God.

When Adam and Eve sinned in the garden, the relationship between God and man was broken.

Only through Jesus Christ, is salvation made available to us.

When we repent by changing our minds to turn away from the sin that separates us from God, and ask for God's forgiveness, we are forgiven by him and receive the right to stand before him, guiltless, through Christ.

Salvation is a gift from God. We receive it only by faith.

3). EDUCATION:

(Proverbs 22:6) (KJV),

Train up a child the way he should go, when he is old, he will not depart from it.

The curriculum I was taught in elementary school has changed to reflect the mindset and views of our current world.

My elementary classroom started each day with prayer, and citing The Pledge of Allegiance to our United States flag.

The curriculum was written with moral concepts. Teachers and principles cared for each child, as their own.

Kids respected authority. When they didn't, teachers and principals were allowed to make them.

Today, we see the total opposite.

Prayer is no longer allowed in our schools.

At an early age, the learning curriculum is tailored to fit immoral lifestyles, accepted by our current society.

With Satan's intent, to plant demonic seeds of rebellion in the hearts of our children at a young age. Ultimately to destroy them.

Most teachers are underpaid and are teaching only for a paycheck. Children no longer respect those in authority.

To the point of bringing weapons to school. With the intent to use them.

Metal detectors now have to be installed in our schools, to enable a safe environment for our children to learn.

Enough is enough! It's time for the church and people of God to wake up!

If we don't get it together, what will happen to our children? The next generation.

We must go back to our spiritual foundation. Those moral traditions handed down from our grandparents, big moma, those church mothers, deacons and pastors, that genuinely cared about our children and did what was necessary to make a difference in their lives.

Their Godly principles taught our children the importance of respecting our elders. Responding to our elders; with yes mam and no sir.

If you made a promise, to always keep it, because having integrity and keeping your word meant everything.

Having a good work ethic, that enables you to provide and support your family.

Not be dependent on handouts from our governmental system, in the form of the welfare, or "stimulus" checks.

It's time we make a change and be about God's business.

4). ARTS:

Look at this beautiful world we live in.

Only God, the master architect and creator, could have designed such beauty.

(Exodus 35:35),(NIV),

States,

He has filled them with skill to do all kinds of work as engravers, designers, embroiderers, in blue, purple, and scarlet yarn and fine linen.

God has equipped us all, with every skill and ability, we need to fulfill the destiny and purpose he's assigned us.

Let's use our gifts and talents for his glory.

5). ENTERTAINMENT:

Most people assume that the Christian life is boring and dull. Not true.

Man made, religious rules, have caused people to turn away from God and the church, to seek entertainment from the world.

God gave us specific instructions on how to entertain ourselves, as Christians.

(Phillippians 4:8) (KJV),

Finally, brothers and sisters, whatever is noble, whatever is right, whatever is pure, whatever is lovely, whatever is admirable. Think about things that are excellent and worthy of praise.

If God assigned you to work in the world of entertainment, seek his guidance on how to create positive, family oriented entertainment, that's pleasing in his sight and will promote his Kingdom agenda.

6). GOVERNMENT:

God provided our governmental system to establish rules, laws, and order on the earth.

Our government leaders are to rule and lead according to biblical principles.

Their rulership should be in the best interest of all people. Not a specific race.

Everyone should be treated fairly. Racism and prejudices of any kind, are purely demonic and should not be tolerated at any level.

Because our God is a God who likes diversity. It's evident with the different races and nationalities he created.

In God's eyes, we're all equal. No race is superior over the other and all lives matter to him.

Corruption in our government and racism, does not go unnoticed by God.

In his timing, he will defend and fight for all people.

All injustices, without repentance, will be punished by him. No one gets by.

Christians are commanded by God to pray for those in authority.

7). FAMILY:

God created the institution of family.

Consisting of a marriage between a man and a woman. From their union, children are born.

God compares marriage to the relationship of Christ and the church.

Parents are instructed by God to teach their children the principles of God's word. To provide an example on how they're supposed to live.

Looking back over my childhood, I've seen the family structure that God intended, drastically changing and slowly disintegrating.

The tv shows I watched growing up; The Waltons, Leave it to beaver and Good Times, exemplified God's view of the family structure.

The families sat down at the dinner table each day and prayed together. They unified together when challenges came.

Real conversations took place and there was a oneness, each family member felt. To help them through life's journey.

Today we see homes being run by single parents, grandparents, two men or two women.

Homosexuality is Satan's demonic attempt, to stop God's original plan, for a man and woman to procreate, and multiply human beings on the earth.

The advancement of technology has caused cell phones and social media to be taken out of context.

Families no longer sit down together and engage conversationally with each other. When they do, everyone is on their cell phone. With minimal or no communication at all.

Our children are consumed with the television and the internet, secretly watching programs parents would never allow them to see. Because we've become too busy with the cares of this life.

We must fight to get our families back because our families represent the church.

When our homes are dysfunctional, so will our churches be.

❦

CHAPTER 3

Walk In Your God Given Destiny And Purpose Being The Authentic Masterpiece God Created You To Be

The definition of authentic is: of undisputed origin; genuine.

Contrary to our current world, that tells us our bodies, created by God, his masterpiece, aren't good enough and to be accepted by our society, we must alter them to fit society's mold.

Satan's lies have caused us to focus more attention on physical beauty, than the spiritual condition of our hearts.

Millions of dollars or more are being spent each year, to embellish and preserve our physical bodies. Which will one day, fade away.

If you're overweight, bald, not happy with the color of your eyes, don't like the size of your body parts.

Having the right amount of money or medical insurance, will allow you to change them.

But why?

(Ephesians 2:10) (KJV), States,

We are God's masterpiece. His handiwork. Made in his image. Not because of any good thing in us, but by his grace.

Through salvation in Christ, our new birth, we become new creations in the sight of God.

The sinful nature we inherited from Adam, that made us a slave to sin, is replaced with the holy and divine nature of God.

Giving us unlimited spiritual authority, everlasting life, and we are empowered to have a prosperous, victorious and blessed life.

We must begin seeing ourselves the way God sees us. Embrace and love ourselves the way he made us.

If it makes you happy to enhance your physical beauty, do it for yourself and not to please others.

If you're fat, skinny or bald, "own it", because you're God's masterpiece. An original that can't be duplicated. God's best work.

Empowered by God almighty, to impact and change the world.

❦

CHAPTER 4

Submit To Your God Given Destiny With Urgency

(Ecclesiastes 3:1) (NIV),

There's a time for everything, and a season for every activity under the heavens,

A time to be born, and a time to die, a and time to plant and a time to uproot,

A Time to kill and a time to heal, a time to tear down and a time to build,

A time to weep and a time to laugh, a time to mourn and a time to dance,

A time to scatter stones and time to gather them,

a time to refrain from embracing,

A time to search and a time to give up, a time to keep and a time to throw away,

A time to tear down and a time to mend, a time to be silent and a time to speak,

A time to love and a time to hate, A time for war and a time for peace, (Ecclesiastes 3:11), (NIV),

He has made everything beautiful in his own time. He has also set eternity in the human heart, no one can fathom what God has done from the beginning to the end.

(Ecclesiastes 3:12), (NIV),

Know that there's nothing better for people than to be happy and do good while they live.

(Ecclesiastes 3:13), (NIV),

That each of them may eat and drink and find satisfaction in all their toil.

This is the gift of God.

One day, our assignment on earth will end.

After you and I take our last breath, we will stand in the presence of Almighty God, our creator.

To give an account for the life we lived while on earth.

If we've accepted Jesus Christ as our Lord and Savior, we won't be judged for our sins, but we will be rewarded by God.

If we reject Jesus, we will be judged by him, at the judgement seat of Christ; The great white throne judgement.

The final judgement prior to the loss being cast into the lake of fire.

Knowing this truth, everyday we wake up, should be lived with Kingdom purpose and intention.

Loving and valuing our beautiful family and loved ones.

Purposely eating right and exercising to destress and remove the toxins from our bodies; God's temple. To ensure our bodies are healthy to fulfill our God given destiny and purpose.

Spreading the love of Christ by showing love and kindness to others.

Spending time in prayer and fasting and reading God's word, to strengthen our spirit.

Taking time to live life and laugh, laugh, laugh!! Proverbs 17:22, (KJV),

States,

A merry heart doeth good like medicine, but a broken spirit drieth the bones.

Laughter is good for the soul.

One of my happy childhood memories is of my daddy, (Sonny Boy, Cochran), making my mom, (Helen Louise, Cochran), laugh.

When daddy wanted to see her laugh, he would pin her down and begin to tickle her until she laughed uncontrollably.

No matter what my sisters and I were doing inside of the house, we would stop and join in on the fun.

It wasn't long before we all would start laughing too.

Laughter is contagious and it does great things for our physical bodies when we laugh.

When we laugh, endorphins are released in our brain. Causing us to feel happy and relaxed. Removing our anxiety. Allowing us to be free and have mental clarity.

They're people all around us crying inside for a glimmer of hope, to life's challenges and disappointments.

Living life angry, short tempered and ready to explode.

The solution they need is a personal relationship with Jesus Christ. Our way maker, comforter and peace. The only hope for our dying world.

Christians must display and extend the love of Christ to others.

Children of God, stop living life and just existing. Begin walking in the freedom that Jesus Christ died on the cross to give you.

You're the only one who can complete the assignment that God gave you to fulfill.

You've got this!

Jesus Christ loves you and he will help you.

CHAPTER 5

Embrace Your Destiny And Purpose By Walking In Your Spiritual Authority

Luke 10:19, *(KJV),

Behold, I give unto you power to tread on serpents and scorpions, and over all the power of the enemy; and nothing shall by any means hurt you.

Let me break it down for you.

As a blood washed believer in Jesus Christ; a child of God, when we're walking in obedience to God's word and living our lives to please him, God and all of heaven backs us.

No weapon the enemy formed against us, will prosper.

As a child of God, we can be bold as a lion, walking with confidence.

The way George Jefferson, from that popular seventies, tv show, The Jeffersons, walked.

What I loved about George Jefferson is, he was proud of who he was.

He was small in stature, but always walked with attitude; his head held high, shoulders squared, exuding boldness and confidence.

Just like my King of Kings, and Lord of Lords, Jesus Christ. Jesus knew who he was and whose he was.

He confidently carried himself that way. Always walking in power and authority.

Never letting Satan kick him around or punk him!

Everytime Satan tempted Jesus to doubt who he was by speaking lies to him, Jesus boldly rebuked him by speaking the truth of God's word and firmly standing on it.

Christians have that same power through Christ. When we operate in his resurrection power that's on the inside of us, we're unstoppable.

So you and I can walk in our destiny and purpose, with the "SWAG" Jesus Christ gave us.

What's stopping you?

Destiny and purpose is calling your name. It's time you fulfill it.

God's destiny and purpose for your life could be, being a good husband, being a good wife, or raising your children.

Do the thing that God called you to do unto him and to the best of your ability.

❧

CHAPTER 6

Your Destiny And Purpose Is Because Of God's Amazing Love For His People

Before you and I ever committed one sin, by missing the mark of God's standard, God loved us and had a plan to redeem us back to him.

John 3:16 (KJV),

States,

God so loved the world, he gave his only begotten son that whosoever believeth in him, should not perish but have everlasting life.

In the story of Hosea and Gomer, God named their children

names with symbolic meaning. Reflecting the relationship between him and Israel.

He called Hosea's first son, Jezreel; named after a place; a valley of that name.

His second child, a daughter, called Lo-Ruhamah; that explained the ruined condition of the kingdom of Israel, and

A second son, Lo-Ammi; as a reminder of God's rejection of his people.

God loves us. Even when we sin and turn away from him, to worship other gods.

We will never understand the depth of God's love for us.

Psalm 8:4-6, (kJV),

What is man, that you are mindful of him? and the son of man, that thou visitest him? For thou hast made him a little lower than the angels, and hast crowned him with glory and honour. Thou madest him to have dominion over the works of thy hands; thou hast put all things under his feet.

Because God is love, he requires us to show that same unconditional love to our brothers and sisters in Christ.

In Hosea 3:1,(KJV),

God illustrates the depth of his love for Israel, when he tells Hosea to buy Gomer back from the slave market.

After she committed adultery, with different men.

This was God's example to Israel, demonstrating his love for them, as they continued to serve other Gods.

God's love for us is so radical, there's no limit to how far he will go to reach us.

His powerful love, for us, causes him to hunt us down with a vengeance. Like a fierce bounty hunter.

God's love for us will bring him to the nightclub to find us.

God's love for us will remove the desire for that drug addiction we could never break, and call us out of a drug house. Never to return again.

God's great love for us will remove our desire and taste for alcohol.

God's love for us will take away a gambling addiction that's destroying our life.

God's love for us will pull us down from a stripper pole. Out of a defiled bed, with a homosexual, and lesbian lover, that we think we can't live without.

God's love for us will call us out of an ungodly relationship, we're "shacking up" in.

God's love for us will cleanse and remove a lying and gossiping tongue.

God's amazing love for his people will break every chain that has us bound.

Running into his arms pleading; Lord, Lord, Lord, what must I do to be saved?

That's the depth of our awesome God's love, for you and I.

CHAPTER 7

Your Destiny Is Apart Of That Great Revival Prior To Christ's Return

The state of sin in our world has morally desensitized us.

What's morally wrong according to God's principles; the bible, is now considered right, in the eyes of our society.

The church of God is neither hot or cold. Revelation 3:16, (KJV),

So then because thou art lukewarm, neither hot or cold, I will spue thee out of my mouth.

If we are not wholeheartedly committed to God, he will reject us.

It's time we individually examine the spiritual condition of our hearts and align ourselves with the word of God.

Acts 2:17, (KJV),

And it shall come to pass in the last days, saith God, I will pour out my spirit upon all flesh: and your son and your daughters shall prophesy, and your young men shall see visions, and your old men shall dream dreams.

Spiritual blindness is the only way we can't see that we're living in the last days.

Before the return of Christ, to rapture his church.

We need spiritual revival to save the hurting and lost. Revival begins individually with you and I.

In these last days, God is going to use spiritual vessels who make themselves available to be used by him.

It matters not if you've been saved; (a born again believer), fifty years, or one day. Young or old.

If you're committed to God's Kingdom agenda, and your heart is right, you're God's candidate.

There's a harvest of souls waiting to come into the Kingdom of God.

God is counting on the blood washed believers in Christ, to bring them in.

We must tell the lost about the gospel, the good news of Jesus Christ.

Living our lives daily, according to his word and sharing his love with our families, co-workers,and the people we meet along our way.

If we make ourselves available, the opportunity will always present itself, to minister to someone in need.

In the form of someone needing encouragement and hope.

CHAPTER 8

The Jewish Feasts Of The Lord; God's Destiny And Purpose For His People

(Leviticus 23:4-8) (KJV),

In this text, God told Moses to have the people of Israel set appointed times, a (holy convocation), to meet with him.

To read and understand his laws, so they could apply them to their lives.

1). PASSOVER:

This event, Celebrated God sparing the firstborn of the Israelites, when the Lord smote the land of Egypt, on the eve of the Exodus.

2). UNLEAVENED BREAD:

This celebration was a reminder of the journey of the children of Israel through the wilderness, when following Passover and the Exodus and they ate unleavened bread. God later gave them manna to eat.

3). FEAST OF FIRST FRUITS:

On this day the Israelites were commanded to bring their first fruits of the grapes to the Temple as an offering.

This became an annual celebration.

4). FEAST OF WEEKS OR *(PENTECOST):

A harvest celebration commemorated God's provision for sustaining his people.

5). FEAST OF TRUMPETS:

The Lord's final harvest of souls.

6). YOM KIPPUR *(DAY OF ATONEMENT):

The day the high priest presented animal sacrifices, for the sins of the people.

7). FEAST OF TABERNACLES OR *(FEASTS OF BOOTHS)

This feast is symbolic of Christ's second coming, when he will establish his earthly kingdom.

God's seven, annual feasts, apply to both Jew and Gentile. The Gentile includes you and I.

They reveal bible prophecy, regarding God's plans, regarding the return of our Savior, Jesus Christ, God's plan to redeem mankind, the coming judgement for God's enemies and the establishment of God's Kingdom on the earth.

The first four feasts have been fulfilled.

Passover, Unleavened Bread, Firsts Fruits and The Feasts of Weeks or Pentecost*(The birth of the church).

The last three feasts, (Feasts of Trumpets, Day of Atonement and Tabernacle), will happen in the future.

Between the first four feasts and the last three feasts, contains the "church age" or period of grace.

The Feasts of Tabernacles ushers mankind into the Millennial Age.

These Feasts are significant to us because they are a reminder to us that Jesus is the completeness of God's plan for our redemption.

God never starts anything he does not complete.

The first four feasts came to pass and in God's timing, so will the remaining three.

Believe it or not people, Jesus Christ is soon to return. The question is, are you ready to meet him?

If you don't know him as your personal Lord and Savior, you're not ready to meet him.

God gave us his word so our souls can be spiritually prepared to stand before him.

Jesus Christ is coming back any day to rapture his church. It could happen in the next minute.

(2Peter 3:9), (KJV),

States,

The Lord is not slack concerning his promise, as some men count slackness; but is longsuffering to us, not willing that any should perish, but that all should come to repentance.

It comes down to a personal decision we all have to make.

We either receive Jesus Christ as our Lord and Savior, or we reject him. There's no gray area.

We're either in the Kingdom of God, or we're out.

Choosing not to make that decision to serve Jesus, is making the decision not to serve him.

CHAPTER 9

The Showdown Of All Show Downs Is About To Go Down

---

*(THE RAPTURE OF THE CHURCH)

(1Thessalonians 4:16-17)(NIV),

For the Lord himself will descend from heaven with a shout, with the voice of an archangel, and with the trumpet of God. And the dead in Christ will rise first.

Verse 4:17,

Then we who are alive and remain shall be caught up together with them in the clouds to meet the Lord in the air; and so shall we ever be with the Lord.

After the Rapture of the Church occurs, Christians will be brought before the judgement seat of Christ, to be rewarded for their good works.

There will be tribulation on the earth, against the enemies of God, like never before.

The violence and rage we experienced in our streets, from the results of the Covid-19 pandemic, that caused people to fear running out of food, gas, and toilet paper, is a walk in the park, compared to the lawlessness and destruction that's soon to come on the earth, after the rapture of God's church happens.

At the end of the tribulation, the curse will be removed from the earth. Evil will no longer exist.

There will be a new heaven and earth, where Jesus will establish his Kingdom.

Satan, the Antichrist, will be bound and cast into the lake of fire, along with those who rejected and mocked Jesus Christ.

They will be punished for all eternity. (Romans 14:11), (NKJV),

At the name of Jesus, every knee will bow and every tongue will confess

that Jesus is Lord.

Jesus Christ is coming back like a thief in the night. No one knows the day or hour.

Spiritually, our souls must be ready to go back with Jesus when he comes.

With my spiritual eyes I can see, the return of Jesus Christ is imminent. To Prepare to meet Jesus, pray the sinner's prayer:

Dear Lord Jesus, I know that I am a sinner, and I ask for your forgiveness. I believe you died for my sins and rose from the dead. I

turn from my sins and invite you to come into my heart and life. I want to trust and follow you as my Lord and Savior.

Revelation 19:11-16, (KJV),

Now I saw heaven opened, and behold, a white horse. And he who sat on him was called faithful and true, and in righteousness He judges and makes war.

v.12

His eyes were like a flame of fire, and on his head were many crowns. He had a name written that no one knew except Himself.

v. 13

He was clothed with a robe dipped in blood, and his name is called The Word of God.

v. 14

And the armies in heaven, clothed in fine linen, white and clean, followed Him on white horses.

v. 15

Now out of his mouth goes a sharp sword, that with it He should strike the nations. And He himself will rule with a rod of Iron. He Himself treads the winepress of the fierceness and wrath of almighty God.

v. 16

On his robe and on his thigh he has the name written:

KING OF KINGS AND LORD OF LORDS...

∞

CHAPTER 10

The Marriage Supper Of The Lamb

The Marriage Supper Of The Lamb, will occur after the church is raptured and meet Jesus in the air.

Those who received Jesus Christ as their Lord and Savior, are invited to attend this glorious celebration.

This will be a joyful celebration that takes place on the earth.

During this celebration, the Bridegroom, Jesus Christ, will be honored and exalted because his wedding day has come and his bride is ready.

(Hosea 2:18), (KJV),

When Israel was unfaithful to God because of her adultery with other gods.

God established a new covenant with his people.

This celebration will be the consummation of that new covenant. Jesus Christ died and rose from the dead for his bride, the church.

He prepared and cleansed her sin, stained soul, with his shed blood, at Calvary's cross, making her white as snow.

No cost was too much to aquire his bride. Not even death.

Because of his sacrifice and never ending love for us, Jesus Christ is worthy to be exalted and praised.

Blessed are they which are called unto the Marriage Supper of the Lamb.

You're invited to attend this glorious celebration. Will you be there? God is giving you a personal invitation today.

Please "RSVP"...

God is waiting to receive your response.

ACKNOWLEDGMENTS

Thank you to my Heavenly father for loving and believing in me. I will never fathom your great love for me.

A special thank you to my amazing husband, Pastor, Victor Leonard Barnwell, for being my rock. I can always count on you to be there for me and I am blessed to have a husband like you.

Thank you to my daughter, Blair Nicole, my "mini me, "and my handsome son, Jerry Charles, for blessing my life with your presence. You both were created by God for greatness, and I love you both unconditionally.

Jaylen, Kaylix and Malik, my beautiful grandchildren, may the blessings of God overflow in your life. I love you all.

Alex, Domonique, Mila, Maleah, Victoria, Chapa and Leya. I love and appreciate you all.

Thank you to my parents, Helen Louise and Woodrow Wilson Cochran, for the gift of life and for the wisdom you've imparted into my life.

I am very grateful and blessed to have you as my parents.

Thank you to my beautiful sisters, Jeanette, Sandra *(a.k.a, Ratty), and Shayla Nicole, for your encouragement and love.

Hell Had to Let Me Go vii

Thank you to my brothers-in- law, Tramell Forney and Dexter Wright. I love you both and I'm happy that you're a part of our family.

Thank you to my additional family members and friends, my grandparents, aunts, uncles, and cousins.

Thank you my Spiritual parents, Pastor, Rogerstine Gourdine, and Lady, Nancy, at The Applied Word Ministry, in Yemassee, South Carolina. I will always love and cherish you both for loving me, and for imparting your wisdom and spiritual guidance into my life.

A special thank you to my in-laws, Joseph and Martha Barnwell. I love and

appreciate you both.

Thank you to my precious New Covenant Christian Fellowship Church family. Serving with you is a joy. I love you all. Expect God to do the impossible at New Covenant.

A special thank you to Victoria Gabrielle Chapa, my awesome and creative, Makeup Artist. I love and appreciate you.

Thank you, Lisa White, for your expertise in styling my hair. I love and appreciate you, my friend.

Jason Abbott, my hilarious photographer, it was a joy working with you. Your style is one of a kind when it comes to choosing the perfect pose.

May God bless you all abundantly.

Printed in the United States
by Baker & Taylor Publisher Services